THE POMEGRANATES OF KANDAHAR

Born in 1957, Sarah Maguire has published three previous collections of poetry, *Spilt Milk*, *The Invisible Mender* and *The Florist's at Midnight*, as well as the anthology *Flora Poetica: The Chatto Book of Botanical Verse*. She is the founder and director of the Poetry Translation Centre at SOAS, and was co-translator with Yama Yari of Afghan writer Atiq Rahimi's *A Thousand Rooms of Dream and Fear* (Chatto, 2006). She is the only living English-language poet with a book in print in Arabic. Sarah Maguire has lived all her life in west London.

THE POMEGRANATES OF KANDAHAR

Sarah Maguire

Chatto & Windus
LONDON

Published by Chatto & Windus 2007

2 4 6 8 10 9 7 5 3 1

Copyright © Sarah Maguire 2007

Sarah Maguire has asserted her right under the Copyright, Designs
and Patents Act 1988 to be identified as the author of this work

The publisher would like to thank Faber & Faber Ltd.
for permission to quote from 'The Bee Meeting' by Sylvia Plath.

First published in Great Britain in 2007 by
Chatto & Windus
Random House, 20 Vauxhall Bridge Road,
London SW1V 2SA

www.randomhouse.co.uk

Addresses for companies within The Random House Group Limited
can be found at:
www.randomhouse.co.uk/offices.htm

The Random House Group Limited Reg. No. 954009

A CIP catalogue record for this book
is available from the British Library

ISBN 9780701181314

The Random House Group Limited makes every effort to ensure
that the papers used in its books are made from trees that have been
legally sourced from well-managed and credibly certified forests.
Our paper procurement policy can be found at:
www.randomhouse.co.uk/paper.htm

Typeset by Palimpsest Book Production Ltd, Grangemouth, Stirlingshire

Printed in the UK by CPI Mackays, Chatham, ME5 8TD

For Saadi Yousef

If I stand very still, they will think I am cow parsley

Sylvia Plath, 'The Bee Meeting'

CONTENTS

THE GRASS CHURCH AT DILSTON GROVE

Papered with clay
then seeded with fescue and rye,

the church walls fur
with a soft green pelt,

filaments trying the air
before climbing the light.

The church is damp;
it smells of a tool-shed:

mineral,
soil coating tines and boots,

vegetable, with the sap
of lifted plants.

At sunset
small squares of yellowing sunlight

plot the fading grass
through cross-hatched windows,

loose panes stove in,
the lead curled back.

Memories of redemption
wane in the rafters,

communion forgotten
in the emptied nave,

a mission beached
without a flock,

the lost souls lost
to the docks.

Pebble-dashed agglomerate:
these are the rough-cast walls

of the first concrete church in London.
And now the grass comes home

as a box of green metaphors
opens

while I watch.
How old I have become.

Everything the grass has asked of me,
I have done:

I have taken the grass for my path,
for my playground, and for my bed;

I have named grass seeds,
I have borne volumes of turf;

I know the stuff of clay,
the weight of sods,

the bloom of *Agrostis*
on mended soil.

Everything the grass has asked of me
on this earth, I have done

except give my self
up

except lie
under its sky of moving roots.

COW PARSLEY, BLUEBELLS

for Kathleen Jamie

Waist-height,
clouds of white lace
in the abandoned graveyard,

the delicate,
filigree umbels
matching

the thumbprints of lichen
embroidering the graves.
A deep current of blue

surges below –
bluebells,
moments of sky

fallen,
brief weather
fixed on wet stems,

conjuring a climate
gone from this chill April dusk,
as rain comes, and light fades.

VIGIL

Late June, the night air stitched with the scent of lime-blossoms.
When you left, these trees were bare.

The last swallows at nightfall: their perfect parabolas of hunger and
    grace.
Each year, only days after they have gone, do I notice they have
    gone.

Fox on the path: wild creature, at home on the cusp of the city,
how long will your gaze lock onto my gaze?

I measure out the cloth to sew a new cover for our bed:
the warp and weft of fabric, its journeys, the places we will meet.

My body alive with your voice.
The phone warm in my hand.

Yards away, the alluvium of the Blue Nile plies the White Nile's silt.
Pull your bed into the courtyard and sleep under a blanket of stars.

Leaving Omdurman, the moon journeys northwards. Hours later,
I stand in her platinum light. Searching her face for your face.

PASSAGES

Decree: clear skies
over the heart
of London: cirrus,

nothing less
flaming
the far edge of blueness,

nothing less
marking
the absolute boundaries

of air, of resolution.
A cast of slowing jumbos,
emptied of fuel, begins

the descent:
trawling
the long southern flight path

down into Heathrow.
When the huge wheels
hatch

from that cold,
aluminium belly,
will a petrified figure

plummet down
(this time)
into a carpark,

breath frozen midair,
the rapt human form
congealed

on the landing gear
tossed three miles clear
from touchdown,

from migration?
The big silvered craft
run the gamut of light,

taking in evening
buoyant, journeyed:
pushed to the edge

of the city: now exposed,
with its parcel of lights,
its human freight

inching homewards
through dusk, mid-September,
as fear

slips its cold roots
through the known.
The dull muddied Thames

is full of the equinox,
dragged by the moon
the dun waters

flush to the Barrier:
a ruined city checked,
a whole rumoured ocean

balanced in abeyance.
Tides dissolve memory:
history

loosens its cargoes
into the tides'
heedless swirling,

forgetting,
heading out to the open.
But the silt sifts on,

turning and sorting:
as the docklands drop
out of sight,

cargoless,
trafficless, winches abandoned,
ceilings undone

to the skies.
And the skies are rivers
freighting

the burdens
of rivers: transhumance
precious and raw

now landing on tarmac.
The jets tick
as they cool,

boxes contracting
on earth,
as rivets ease back:

the hulk
emptied of passengers
now filling

with migrants:
labouring in the site
of exile and arrival.

The swallows
left weeks ago,
with no notice:

one afternoon
the skies
were abandoned:

lack
takes them southwards.
And in the formal garden,

the last hybrid roses
flare rose-pink and
salmon and mauve,

but the sap's on the turn.
And the earth is balanced,
day equalling night:

and is equally
unbalanced
as rumours are pieced

into news.
After this: winter.
The youngest vixen repeats

her sharp scent,
doubles back, excited,
back again,

crouching,
back now to the rough path:
slips

under the light paling fence
and is
gone:

SOLSTICE

The solstice sunset of the final summer of this thousand years
finds us silent, side by side, divided by the dateline.

The earth has turned its back: the swollen sun
is swallowed by the dome of the Observatory.

The Thames at Greenwich is a beaten platinum ribbon
coiling through the city, unspooling to the teeming sea.

The rose sky's turning mauve, then violet, then midnight blue.
But look at London kindling the night: each lit light an act of faith.

The grid of it: crossroads, junction boxes, wired-up and fused;
and the trains without drivers are crossing the city all night.

Because I am fallen, I must fly down this hill.
Because I have lost you, I must take up this thread.

COTTON BOLL

From here, the cotton fields stretch further than an ocean,
undulant green, pocked with foam.

Little bush, burning in the catastrophic heat,
how far did you come

to set root in this thick black earth, humidity rising,
staggering belief?

Sheets, winding-sheets, underthings, handkerchiefs –
a polity of garments

spun from that one fine thread, yanked
straight out of your heart.

Dyed, dark-stained with sweat, how invisible is the yarn
that ties the weaver to the woven

when all we grasp is stuff –
the loosening fabric of desire, or of utility,

that we labour to possess, unlace, discard,
then burn.

THE PHYSIC GARDEN

1.

Hard to have faith in these twisted dry sticks
crusted with rime;
hard to believe that roots
still web the blank soil of the Order Beds.
Species and genera,
a crop of old labels bedded in iron
their stalled limbs aimed at an empty sky.

2.

A cold spring, a late spring.
Reticence, patience.

Fresh leaves risk the weather.
The first primrose burns.

All of the daffodils
arrive all at once.

3.

Nothing is written
on the leaves of the bluebell,
blank strips of green
fallen back on the grass.

The flowers cluster and rise:
mute mauve fingerstalls –
a knee-high haze
under sycamore and oak.

4.

Disease infuses
the garden's roses
as a fungus pools
around the stilled blooms.

5.

Look, even in July,
the leaves of the
Liriodendron
are learning to yellow:

lemon and gold
leavening the green.

6.

Someone is burning
the last leaves of autumn.

The veil of sharp musk
unfurls through the shrubbery,

the sweet aroma of loss
stinging tears from my eyes.

7.

This, then, is dusk in the garden:
light fled

to a honeycomb of yellow
where the gardeners have gone

to clean soil from their tools.

8.

Even in the still centre of the high-walled garden
paradise is contingent.

On a bench in the dark
the hurt roar of traffic batters the night;

one jet a minute landing at Heathrow.

9.

Journeys taken so long ago
the seeds sow themselves

turn weedy
                    escape

EUROPE

Merely an idea bruising
the far horizon, as a cold mist tightens into rain –

but at dusk we still wait
by the Bay of Tangier, on the old city walls, gazing northwards

till the night comes on,
and a necklace of lights gathers the throat of the sea.

The young men burn –
lonely, intent on resolving that elusive littoral

into a continent of promises
kept, clean water, work. If they stare hard enough, perhaps

it will come to them.
Each night, they climb these crumbling ramparts

and face north
like true believers, while the lighthouse of Tarifa blinks

and beckons,
unrolling its brilliant pavement across the pitiless Straits.

RAMALLAH

Freezing out of season
with Eid after Easter

– a provisional city
a concatenation

of loose roundabouts
building sites

and razor wire –
scars of forced demolitions

spite
occupation and new wealth

Little Bantustan
rimmed twice with checkpoints

claustrophobia
of the stone's-throw distance

disconnected phone lines
no phone lines

and roads
stopping short

Hard-core and gravel
a job-lot of kerbstones

wires spewing from snowcem
as frozen rain fumes up

the broken street
Rattling windows in the teashop

jammed shut with old rags
steamed-up with the steam

from *chai bi nana*
from the honey tobacco

of ancient *nargilas*
from gossip and politics and love

The dank rotting theatre
perished through

with thirty years of enforced
darkness

Plush slides
off the chairs

dust rots through the curtains
and every human breath

exhales its weather upwards
in a cloud

I never found the centre
just a ring

of handsome policemen
dressed in blue

March, 1997

LANDSCAPE, WITH DEAD SEA

Flat out on brine
    at the bottom of the world –
        not one wisp of cirrus

can mar the lapis lazuli dome
    cupped over this dry bowl of hills,
        pastel hills folded in stillness.

Buoyant on bitterness –
    the tonnage of fluids transfigures
        into haze above my very eyes,

to a mist heavy with elements,
    molecules of sweet water
        shipped up slowly to infinite blue.

These deep, barren waters
    are riddled with toxins and salts.
        At the shoreline I harvest

the dark, sybaritic mud –
    worked into my flesh, its granular
        astringency erodes my dead skin.

Down south, Potash City –
    acres of evaporation pans
        and chimneyed factories,

ringfenced depots stacked up with acids,
    with phosphates in boxes
        and sulphurous drums.

At sunset, the western, volatile sky
    ebbs through carmine into mauve.
            The lights come on in Jericho:

I imagine what I cannot see –
    barbed wire threaded with jasmine,
            sharp enough to smell.

This riven land: here
    the great tectonic plates glide asunder
            as fast as my fingernails grow,

riding the molten core of magma –
    the invisible, radiant heart of the earth,
            burdened by geography, charged with life.

THE *SAND FULMAR*

Squat, the flat shade of sand–
flats, docked west of Woolwich,

the *Sand Fulmar* waits
to be emptied:

of silt, of erosion, of friable shale
bled down to riverbeds:

a mobile geography
shipped from estuary to factory.

After twelve days
all the grains are spooned

clear of the hull,
crowning a huge mounting dune

crawling up skywards.
Tonight,

the full hull of the dredger
is heavy as a river:

the Thames elbows its flanks
and streams on.

A school of orange buoys
winks, as the high Thames churns

seawards:
burst flowers of lights

bloom and split
while the tide plies the currents:

but the dredger won't budge,
absorbed with its load,

silt
hoarded up to its gills.

Two big cartwheels of paddle flats
with rough shovels attached

plunged deep under water,
hauling marl

from slowed sand-banks,
brackish juices

spilling down
the chins of the buckets,

set free to flow onwards,
lured by the undertow.

Now, at the depot's edge,
soft migrant grains

will bed down in darkness,
a promiscuous mingling

of mica and silica,
of small bones and smashed shells,

of beachglass and rock quartz,
with sandworms,

with seaweeds
torn up from their roots.

Once the huge tube is screwed
into place

the granular cargo
is parcelled along

a once–cream–painted
busted and rusting conveyorbelt

twenty yards high,
to dust the new landscape

mounting behind the locked chainlink fence.
In the factory of aggregates

tall vats of spent oil
stand by shy growths of ragwort

or rosebay willowherb,
the sharp tang

of coaltar staining the air.
These are the journeys

of the slow hearts of rivers
turned stubborn with silt:

dredged clear, transported,
they will curdle in bitumen.

Sealed drums of asphalt,
stirred into pitch and mixed up with sand,

wait to be fired,
to be laid down as roads.

THE FOOT TUNNEL

for Andrew

The dream always dreamt just before dawn:
walking the cool white tunnel to its end,
pace echoing pace,

the chill white tiles streaming with breath,
with rumours of the Thames
(its brown tons of water and cargoes,

its river creatures, silt) dragging above us,
pointing the walls with a century of damp.
We pass through a ghost-mist, drawn on

by a row of dim lamps pinned to the ceiling
pulling us downwards through walled-up clay
deep underneath the cold throat of the river.

Spilt out of the wood-panelled, rickety lift
we are shocked by air, by seagulls soaring and diving,
by the world swivelled round, clouds, the sudden

smell of the sea. We have walked under
water, to be drenched to the bone
by a joyful June downpour, punched from the skies.

MY FATHER'S PIANO

Carved from the seasoned hearts of rosewood –
    the fine grain veined black
        through the sheen of maroon –
    my father's piano
        was the centre of home;

the sounding-board of thought and feeling
    ignited by
        the heartbeat, heartbeat, heartbeat
    threading through the scales
        of pitch in time.

Look at it unpacked –
    a junction box of forged connections,
        the waves of felts
    in red and green and deep sky blue,
        the interleaved shanks,

the hammers and dampers, stacked and packed in
    as close as a skeleton,
        stitched through with steel –
    the plumblines of tension –
        the strings spun around

their curved constellation of chromium pins
    scattered on a sky
        gilded Krugerrand gold.
    Always I was staggered
        by the deep bass darkness

catching at my heart, resounding around
    my lungs and bones,
        by the tinsel glissando
    housed in high ivories
        at the edge of sound –

the hammers' attack on the strings forging joy,
    then tempering tenderness.
        This is the work of love –
    the testing of harmonies
        through the risk

of dissonance, trying again as the hands fall apart,
    taking on silence
        when the afternoon fades –
    practice and grace,
        as light ebbs away before tea.

IN PASSING

I cannot now remember
    how I came to be waiting
        on a bench in a car park

at the back of a station
    in the suburbs of Philadelphia
        twenty-six years ago −

strange, American weeds
    lifting the pocked asphalt,
        a mongrel asleep in a rusting trolley,

the tired light a hive of dust motes
    thronging the limp damp air
        of a late August heatwave.

I had never been alone,
    so far from home, before,
        observer of these passing,

ordinary lives − the wonder
    of finding myself, here,
        out of place, unobserved.

I stepped on the platform
    just as a goods train passed through.
        The length of it winded me −

boxcar after boxcar after boxcar
    furiously intimate, close enough to touch:
        the whiplash of turbulence,

the aftershock of silence.

COIL

Ash, a drained glass half-kissed,
a cache of spent razorblades –

relics, evidence I steel myself to clear away.

And the one coil of hair I found in our sheets?
That, I took on my tongue.

TO DAMME AND BACK

Pacing the towpath of the straight canal,
　　once a highway for cloth of gold,
　　　　wool bales, bolts of lace,

now slowed to the traffic of waterfowl,
　　squabbling mallards,
　　　　and paired, reflective swans.

Drawn by perspective the water arrows
　　clean to its vanishing point,
　　　　ruled by two unbroken rows

of leafless poplars, elegant cages of opalescent air,
　　while a soft haze cures the unspoken waters,
　　　　a seam of silver threading these rich,

alluvial soils – polderland at peace on Easter Sunday.
　　Damme: once a frantic harbour, next a backwater
　　　　beached by the slow accretions of silt,

now safe with streets of steep-gabbled houses,
　　their clean rooms lined with fine china and books,
　　　　overlooking cobblestones polished with mist.

The squat gothic church is shut –
　　rooks absolving the huge silenced belfry,
　　　　the gathering bats, gravestones of infants.

We turn round at dusk, walking the known path
　　into darkness, retracing the trees, counting
　　　　our steps into five long kilometres,

the freight of ourselves bearing our return – worn bones,
full lungs, the finite heart, these intricate networks
of balance and loss carrying us back

as the night turns chill. Side by side our journeys
divide – youth draws you on, but now
I am taking the old path home.

WINTERING IN TANGIER

for Mimi Khalvati

Here, even in winter, the hibiscus blooms burn,
scarlet, cerise, tangerine –

random flares
starring the rough, boxy hedgerows (dark-leaved, evergreen)

that guide these small sideroads
down to the sea.

Or in the shrubbery of a garden overlooking
the Bay of Tangier,

the very last flowers
observe the mild air, their sere petals the fabric of skin.

Neither fallen nor saved,
I am wintering with the grasses –

examining the troubled lawn,
or wandering through a forest of the huge globed heads

of papyrus,
lost beneath a high mist of teased grasshair

netted with dew.
Perhaps I could split

their sharp, triangular stems into strips
and splice them into poetry.

A BOWL OF TRANSVAAL DAISIES

for Seitlhamo Motsapi

Time darkens the petals
from scarlet to madder,

the plush fringe of lashes
curling backwards,

brittle rims
latching onto air

onto oxygen,
tenderly fingering the white china bowl –

a last,
vagrant gesture.

★   ★   ★   ★

When you entered my bedroom
they were erect,

tall
in the tall cool vase,

their long, slender stems
drinking, drinking –

pliant necks spooling up
into the shocked high rush

of red mouths wide open
in joy, in astonishment.

★   ★   ★   ★

Ten flat wheels of redness,
hot feathers

spooling
from the spun hub of gold.

Small planets fallen to earth,
they shoulder

the grass
and fire into light,

fat pollen shaking
its thick yellow blessings on the wind.

★   ★   ★   ★

I came back
to a cold place,

crockery stacked in the sink,
chairs pushed back from the table,

your book propped open.
The gerberas were falling –

heavy heads keeling downwards,
kissing the china,

their soft useless necks
gone, all over.

★   ★   ★   ★

I slit their throats –
ten of them,

right through the core.
Fed them to a flat china bowl

as they jostled the whiteness
and gazed aloft.

A forest of soft eyes open below me,
memory pulsing the fading red veins,

the curved fabric hardening
into a map.

*   *   *   *

A bowl of Transvaal daisies
waning at dusk,

releasing the tincture
of over, a slight fug staining the air.

I am exhausted by relics,
by this beautiful display

of loss and dust.
Please come here and tell me

their ten red names,
Gerbera jamesonii, moarubetso, beloved.

STEADFAST

The heart of Everest
is studded
with corals,

small shells and liverwort,
sea creatures
petrified

Friable limestone,
its crystals
erode

under snow, come adrift
in the blue,
leavening air

The ocean, my love,
is truly very shallow –
it ships mountains

up
from its flanks,
forests, lagoons

What is steadfast
is moving –
time weathered in stone,

salts
laid down in sediment,
leaf fall,

the hard push of buds,
in rain
beating the glass

A FISTFUL OF FORAMINIFERA

Sand, at first glance –
granular,

a rich grist
of grains and slim seeds,

opening
into a swarm of small homes

painted rose or ochre, saffron, chalk,
some blown steady as glass –

hyaline, diamond,
the pellucid private cradle of a tear.

*　　　*　　　*　　　*

The balanced simplicity of a singlecelled cell,
busy with its business

in absolute silence.
Pseudopodia

float
clear through their apertures,

banners coursing the waters,
furbelows, scarves, ragged skirts;

brief tactful netting,
shy gestures of touch.

Their filigree mansions
are chambered with secrets –

auricular passageways
give onto galleries,

soft arcades,
furrowed with arbours, open

onto balconies, that lean
over doors, propped ajar.

*   *   *   *

Benthic,
their galaxies carpet the depths of the oceans,

a slow chalky ooze
bedded down softly in darkness.

They conjure their houses
from flotsam and jetsam,

tucking grains closely
between alveoli,

secreting a hardy, calcareous mortar;
the shell walls buffed till they shine

or pebbledashed sugary white –
the architectonics of happenstance and grace.

*   *   *   *

Pennies from heaven,
the yellowing bedrock

hewn into slabs
is stuffed full of treasures.

Slipped from their homes
come hundreds of coins,

big stumbling sovereigns,
pocketfuls of pocketmoney,

fit for flipping, fit for hoarding
in chests.

Nummulites gizahensis,
the wealth of the pharaohs

is hauled up heavenwards,
a limestone staircase to the stars.

★   ★   ★   ★

Tumbleweeds, spacecraft, seedpearls, squid,
fairylights, pincushions, biodomes, sheaths,

colanders, starfish, thistledown, dhal,
powderpuffs, ammonites, cornichons, teeth,

puffballs, longbones, condoms, bulbs,
thermometers, pomegranates, catapults, hail.

★   ★   ★   ★

Open your fists
and the mortal remains of one million creatures

will spill
through your fingers —

Eocene
dust in the wind.

THE WATER DIVINER

Under the last shade of the pine trees
they wait together in silence
while he roams their wasted land –
a sleepwalker, driven, entranced.
Heat summons up dust devils
from the parched floor of the valley,
banners of sand unrolling in the breeze.

Who could remember water
in the face of this cracked earth –
scarred by dark fissures,
a hard web of desiccation
transfixed by the skulls of dry gourds
sprawling hollowed where they fell,
by the scorched hulls of fruit trees,
by the scratched evidence of grass?

Beneath soil turned to dust,
beneath the implacable bedrock,
he knows sweetness courses.
Pliancy babbling in darkness,
a wet ore threading through
potholes and boulders,
an aquifer swollen and cool.

His indigo robes seek out
their element, his wandering path
mimics a river in spate
chancing a new route to flood.
He balances the sappy twig
of precious hazelwood,
a hair-trigger sprung wetly green
under the peeled-back bark.

A slim boy in blue measuring a wasteland,
as if his feet could mend the torn soil
he walks the dried grid of the land,
conjuring liquid, his murmured prayers
big raindrops kicking up dust,
wanting an echo. But the level
branch holds as he paces the distance.

Dusk is coming. Then suddenly –
the sapling spasms and tears
from his grasp, and the water-diviner
faints where he stands. And now
he is a door opened on wetness.
He is a full well plumbed deep
underground. He is fodder for cattle.
An orchard in bloom.

THE POMEGRANATES OF KANDAHAR

The bald heft of ordnance
A landmine
shrapnel cool in its shell

Red balls
pinioned in pyramids
rough deal tables stacked to the sky

A mirrored shawl
splits
and dozens tumble down –

careering through the marketplace
joyful fruit
caught by the shouts of barefoot children

Assembled, they are jewels –
jewels
of garnet, jewels of ruby

A promise deep as the deep red of poppies
of rouged lips (concealed)
Proud hearts

built of rubble
Come, let us light candles in the dust
and prise them apart –

thrust your knife through the globe
then twist
till the soft flesh cleaves open

to these small shards of sweetness
Tease each jellied cell
from its white fur of membrane

till a city explodes in your mouth
Harvest of goodness,
harvest of blood

PETERSBURG

for Ruth

A week with no stars.
A week with the full moon blinded by light.

At midnight, the Winter Palace is on fire –
one thousand molten windows

scarlet with the agonies of sunset
igniting in the west.

I run across the Palace Bridge
into the origin of red,

intent on the bloodied winding cloth
of a day that's refusing to die.

City giddy with light,
balancing water with granite,

urgent with traffic pounding
this bridge that, soon, will throw up its arms

to let the night ships glide to the north,
heavy with exchange.

City of ghosts, familiars, lyrics –
and words, mouthed into stone.

Transparent Petropolis, absolute beauty
is a shard of glass snagging the heart –

the subjects of imperial architecture
are cancelled by the fury of scale.

These infinite vistas master the Neva
in a hard embrace – its bedrock

the countless hands of slaves,
impossibly gilded, furnishing the swamp.

This is the illusion: perspective is everything.
Wherever I may stand,

the vanishing point is my eye,
the beholden.

THE JARDIN DES PLANTES

Do not go to the Jardin des Plantes.
The false acacia has shed all its leaves.
The cedar is threadbare. The avenue
of lime-trees is an avenue of stumps,
lopped limbs prickling with hapless twigs.

Do not go to the Jardin des Plantes.
Instead, stay here by the river.
Stay here and keep vigil for that man
on the Right Bank who is losing his mind.
There, at the lip of the Seine, beneath

the oblivious, continuous traffic,
watch him pace his stone stage, half-naked
at freezing point, haranguing his invisible familiars,
beating the insensible concrete with his fists.
January. The river cold as a blade.

The suffocated sky like cotton-wool wadding.
Stay here and watch. Kneeling, then flailing
at the wall. Beseeching the water. No one
knows you are here, observing a stranger
in agony across the river. Do not go

to the Jardin des Plantes. The cactus house
is closed. The order beds are bald.
The rheumy-eyed pansies leak back into the soil.
Little cloches abound, cosseting the feeble
under sweating, grime-streaked panes of glass.

Meanwhile, there is gravel. Meanwhile,
everything you love is staked up, cut back or
dead. And now the wind is a weapon.
The weather is a weapon.
A basketful of knives spat in your broken face.

Alone in a city of pursed lips, abandoned by a river
that knows nothing of the tides, a river
unlatched from the moon, a river too far from the sea.
So face the implacable river, Left Bank/Right Bank.
Face that man a hundred yards off, that stranger

cursing this bitter dusk.
Do not go to the Jardin des Plantes.
Stay here on these steps till darkness is absolute,
till nothing can be seen of that figure at the river's edge,
a woman eclipsed.

TOTAL ECLIPSE

I have travelled this far: to a stubbled field in a foreign land;
the heavens above, a cold bowl full of clouds.

We are pilgrims seeking portents through the prisms of science.
Earthbound: the sucking clay soil doubles my boots.

Eclipsed: abandoned. The unpredicted has finished my heart.
And the weather itself will brook no prediction.

Seconds away, a black tornado is scouring the earth.
No revelation: just absolute darkness at half-past noon.

The dead cells of my eyes double and swarm, seeding the clouds
as the inexorable calendar ticks through my heart.

I submit my evidence: of what I could not see coming.
I recall my memory: of what is finished.

WOLVES ARE MASSING ON THE STEPPES OF KAZAKHSTAN

Close to home, their prints
darken the snow.

Come full moon,
the whole night is anguished –

cattle
stagger in their sheds

knocking the walls,
churning fodder and litter;

wide-eyed in lamplight
they buck and bruise.

Under Stalin
culls worked like clockwork –

wolves skinned from their pelts
were hung out to dry,

as cotton stretched to new horizons,
as Kazakhs ate the dust.

Now fences are mended
bolts shot home

and the shotgun propped
by the bed

is oiled and loaded.
But sleep, sleep is fitful

as the wolf packs mass
on the steppes of Kazakhstan.

A VILLAGE OF WATER

At first it was as though
it had rained all night.
When we woke
the gutters were full,
the cobblestones dark,
slippery to walk across
as we carried all we could carry
further up the hillside,
making odd camps of possessions,
parking them higgledy-piggledy
under the shade
of the tall cedar trees,
to be taken away
far over the mountains.

Water seeks its own level.
The cart-ruts filled,
cow dung formed stepping stones,
children splashed in new pools,
excited to watch how they'd swell,
spill rivulets, form ponds,
then miniature lakes.
After a week, in the centre of our village
the alleys were all slurry.
Once the carpets that we wove
cast a deep lake of rainbows
across the floor of the mosque.
Now God has spilt us a mirror
that, like us, ascends to paradise, slowly.

Thigh-deep in water,
we passed our lives from hand
to hand, a chain-link of arms
bearing haybales and crockery,
wedding dresses, shovels and pots.
Each day four more fingers of water
edged up the doorstops,
spilling over kerbstones,
seeping through the rough
Hessian sandbags stitched
by my grandmother, patiently,
as though she were sewing her shroud,
tight seams sealing flesh from the cold,
until rot does its work.

The courtyard was ruined,
the kitchen flags awash,
the hearthplace sodden,
the stairs led down to a pond.
Unhinged by the currents,
windows filled with the image
of their element.
What we have abandoned
discovers the grace of fluency.
Things would wobble a little,
then lose their grip, kick off, float.
The intimate detritus
of a broken-backed chair,
a buoyant shirt, a kettle upsidedown.

We camped out in the barn,
waiting for the future.
A lonely ark, our animals
rubbing at the walls.
Next day, they penned us in carts
beside them, jeering, cuffing us
for speaking our mother-tongue.
We looked back to watch
our lives drown beneath us:
a village of water.
An archipelago of citrus trees
and chimneys, sinking,
then swallowed.
Only the minaret pointing to heaven.

DAMASCENE

Centuries of barefoot pilgrims have walked
this white marble to the stuff of glass –

billowing, doubled in *hijab*, I look down
into the heavens' absolute descent.

Swarming aloft from the rink of the Umayyad Mosque
a dark crowd of pigeons rips

open the fabric of dusk –
figures scaling the last slow heat of September,

a heat heavy with the end of a summer's summer –
its dust now settling onto cupolas and pantiles,

onto the balconied, octagonal minaret
where Jesus, one day, will alight to bring Judgement.

In the greenish, underwater gloom of the Prayer Hall
the head of John the Baptist waits behind bars.

   ★   ★   ★   ★

How strange I am to myself here –
out of bounds, unknown.

Lost in the night streets of Damascus
I am a figment of shadows

cast by yellowing lamps
down pleated corridors of overlapping homes;

their whitewashed flanks are still warm from the sun –
breathing, intricate, woven from wattle and thatch.

★   ★   ★   ★

In a room walled with carpets,
a room warm with the smell of shorn wool

and the metallic tincture of dyes –
he laid me on a *kilim*, and I bled.

FROM DUBLIN TO RAMALLAH

for Ghassan Zaqtan

Because they would not let you ford the river Jordan
and travel here to Dublin, I stop this postcard in its tracks –
before it reaches your sealed-up letterbox, before yet another
   checkpoint,
before the next interrogation even begins.

And instead of a postcard, I post you a poem of water.
Subterranean subterfuge,
an indolent element that slides across borders,
as boundaries are eroded by the fluency of tongues.

I send you a watery bulletin from the underwater backroom
of Bewley's Oriental Café,
my hands tinted by stainedglass light as I write,
near windows thickened with rain.

I ship you the smoked astringency of Formosa Lapsang
   Souchong
and a bun with a tunnel of sweet almond paste
set out on a chipped pink marble-topped table,
from the berth of a high-backed red-plush settle.

I greet you from the ranks of the solitary souls of Dublin,
fetched up over dinner with the paper for company.
Closer to home and to exile,
the waters will rise from their source.

I give you the Liffey in spate.
Drenched, relentless, the soaked November clouds
settle a torrent of raindrops
to fatten the flood.

Puddles pool into lakes, drains burst their sides,
and each granite pavement's slick rivulet has the purpose of
    gravity.
Wet, we are soaking in order to float.
Dogs in the rain: the cream double-decker buses steam up and
    stink

of wet coats and wet shopping,
a steep river of buses plying the Liffey;
the big circumnavigations swing in from the suburbs, turn,
cluster in the centre, back off once more.

Closer to home and to exile:
I seek for this greeting the modesty of rainwater,
the wet from ordinary clouds
that darkens the soil, swells reservoirs, curls back

the leaves of open books on a damp day into rows of tsunami,
and, once in a while, calls for a song.
I ask for a liquid dissolution:
let borders dissolve, let words dissolve,

let English absorb the fluency of Arabic, with ease,
let us speak in wet tongues.
Look, the Liffey is full of itself. So I post it
to Ramallah, to meet up with the Jordan,

as the Irish Sea swells into the Mediterranean,
letting the Liffey
dive down beneath bedrock
swelling the limestone aquifer from Hebron to Jenin,

plumping each cool porous cell with good Irish rain.
If you answer the phone, the sea at Killiney
will sound throughout Palestine.
If you put your head out the window (avoiding the snipers,
    please)

a cloud will rain rain from the Liffey
and drench all Ramallah, drowning the curfew.
Sweet water will spring from your taps for *chai bi nana*
and not be cut off.

Ghassan, please blow up that yellow inflatable dinghy stored
   in your roof,
dust off your compass,
bring all our friends,
and swim through the borders from Ramallah to Dublin.

ADEN

After the apocalyptic
crack!
and bolt of light,
there's the slowing hum

in the blackened room
of the ceiling fan
ticking itself
right down

to a standstill.
Machines gone:
the soft tidal roar
of the air-conditioner's

absence
leaves the dark agape indoors:
absorbed in detail,
with the smallest pitch

of movement,
(cloth on skin),
(a lizard's footprints
up the wall),

as the night outside
comes in:
the insistent scratching
of cicadas

backing for
the distant heated voices;
while an empty breeze
lifts the wet ears

of banana leaves
and lets them flop.
In the street
the severed snake of cable

slumps across
the pockmarked tarmac,
its heart
a bristling mesh

of wires and sinews
jutting
from the torn-up stump,
spilling volts

into the open road.
Hotter than a London heatwave,
the wild clouds boil
across the moonlit sky.

Everyone's gone home to bed.
Outside the
British Council bungalow
we guard the cable,

keeping watch
on peeling plastic
kitchen chairs.
But no-one needs protecting:

even the scrawny cats
slink off,
deaf to our calls,
disinterested, aloof.

GLAUCIUM FLAVUM

Yolk broken on the shingle,
a cadmium flag –
five silken petals
flourished by a sharp November breeze.

Beached on detritus,
sheltered by the litter of Seablite and Stonecrop,
the Yellow Horned-poppy
finds shelter on rubble,

harvesting moisture
from dewdrops latched between stones.
Split, the plant exudes
a toxic yellow gum,

that's stowed in hirsute leaves
against the saline plague of the sea.
Its seed pod, a curved, black bean,
is a torn claw, vacant

as winter knuckles down.
Beyond Thorpeness
rear the bulbous, concrete tanks of Sizewell,
hatching reactions, collisions,

staining the tides with their alien warmth.
Yet still the sea repeats
its old declensions,
rubbing armfuls of flints into grit,

then sand,
making dust to be swept off by winds
when the land is barren
and the coastline gone.

HUNGER

Our lust for swollen purple aubergines,
their taut and glistening skins
and the smoky flesh within –

a chilli–dotted, slow-braised hotpot from Szechwan,
and whole, bitter, baby *brinjal*, curried with dahl,
and disks, dusted with spices, grilled *al-sudani* –

provoked a sudden hunger on Regent Street at midnight,
and your soft mouth on mine, upstairs on the nightbus,
tasting me, all the way home.

THE BOWL OF MILK

(After Pierre Bonnard)

I balance the bowl of milk
perfectly, head up,
crossing the cool kitchen flags,

the lip of the meniscus
creaming the thick china rim
as I move. The cat's tongue

draws me, his rough suck lapping,
lapping at his drink.
Somnambulist in moonlight,

I am managing solitude,
solitude and fur – the primed
muscles of a throbbing tail

curled round cold furniture,
the lithe pelt that longs to be stroked.
In this light, at this hour,

shadows are exact, cut and boxed,
but my dress turns puce.
I would mention this jug

of oriental poppies, the tincture
coming from their dark, open mouths,
but what lies at the heart of them?

PSORIASIS

If a red rose lies at the heart of me,
it cannot bloom.

Speechless, unknown –
but for this roseate

plague on my knuckles
and knees,

shedding its bastard pollen
in my sheets;

colourless,
the wrong pain.

FEBRIFUGE

Your burning brow.
Your skin a skin of wet and salt.

Waiting until waiting
becomes an hallucination of waiting.

Like the aftershock of a tuning fork
lifted, struck and held.

That doubleness.
That other realm.

Or glass –
then void and only the ashen remains.

What could ache mean
except something intrinsic

to the length,
to the pull of longbones?

Dud bitterness
of the hollow tongue and its attendants.

Vital acids swilling
in the faded china bowl.

A blessing:
the cool and clarity of folded linen;

the heads of meadowsweet;
the inner bark of osiers and willows.

.

Two tiny printed cakes of aspirin
flame inside the glass,

a veil of whiteness
fuming through the water.

REFLECTION

Occluded moon. A tattered coat of wild clouds flails across the sky.
Rest is fugitive, my love, if departure is your destination.

Because I have seen the blossoming wisteria reflected in your eyes
my grief is doubled now its spent lilac petals lie scattered on the
   ground.

Everything that occurred was recorded in this mirror.
But only in darkness can I see your reflection next to mine.

For one hour at midsummer the sun climbs higher than these
   walls.
And here I am, indoors, in darkness, walled in by sorrow and ink.

The moon is doubled in the Nile, reflected in the Thames.
But look up at her: bone-cold, alone, eternal night at her disposal.

Into whatever language my name may be translated,
my name is solitary. This well of ink will act as my reflection.

FIELD CAPACITY

The plump loam easy with wetness –
late March, the unwrung sponge of soil
balanced by a long winter's rain,
then opened with thaw.

I take the springy lawn in my stride,
an ash sapling tucked under each arm.
A circle described in the turf, the grassy lid
lifted, then dig –

and the packed earth comes nicely,
fresh on the spade. Fed, then watered in darkness,
the rootball unwinds, as the young tree
shivers in the wet spring air.

ALMOST THE EQUINOX

and the Thames so emptied of current
it shows bare flanks of sand. Beige sand. A beach.
The sudden vertigo of hardness when we're cupped
over the walls of the Embankment

examining the strange cream stones below,
driftwood, bottle-tops, crockery, one sodden boot.
And the slow mud opens its mouth.
Jets long departed, their con-trails fire

across the fierce blue skies, unfurling
into breath. The very last weather of a summer
spent impatient for change,
waiting for a sign, an alignment.

Beneath our feet, a hemisphere away,
the full moon tugs fluids into tides, and stops
another night in its tracks,
hours before it climbs over London –

the constant pull of elsewhere
mooring us outside ourselves. The colchicums
come naked into the early autumn air.
Bruised into mauve and purple,

their frail blooms admit the memory of harm
in their risky flight to beauty. Packed bulbs
underground harbour their secrets.
Now that we have witnessed

the flare of that ginkgo spilling up
beside St Paul's – its roots woven
deep beneath a graveyard of graves,
its slim knotted branches, sleeved

with airy, fantail leaves –
it will return to us, suddenly,
years from now. Anomalous Jurassic relic,
its origins are as ancient as these slabs

of blackening Whin-bed Portland Stone,
set here by Wren to stamp out Fire and Plague.
As a child, I climbed all the stairs
to the Whispering Gallery, laid my cheek

against the painted plaster of the dome,
and let those perfected acoustics bear my changed voice
back to myself. The huge nave
reminds you of the Great Mosque in Kabul –

sunlight falling on pillars of stone, the hushed intentness
of prayer. Shattered, war-torn, it's still standing,
somehow, next to the river by the Bridge of Bricks,
just as Wren's great dome once soared above the Blitz,

intact. Tonight, we will look up to see
Mars, that old harbinger of war, come so close to us
it rivets the southern sky with its furious,
amber flare. Sixty-thousand years ago it lit

these heavens and looked down
on ice. Next convergence, nothing will be left of us
leaning on this bridge of wires and tempered steel,
wondering at the river and the city and the stars,

here, on the last hot night before this planet tilts us
into darkness, our cold season underground.
The tide has turned, the Thames comes inching back,
drowning everything it will reveal again.

for Yama

NOTES

The Grass Church at Dilston Grove

In October 2003 the artists Heather Ackroyd and Dan Harvey
created a remarkable installation by sowing grass seeds all over
the walls of the deconsecrated church in Dilston Grove,
Rotherhithe. Formerly the docklands' centre for the mission work
of Clare College, Cambridge, this pioneering concrete structure
was designed in 1911 by Sir John Simpson and Maxwell Ayrton.
Since 1969 the building has acted as a gallery and studio space
for a number of artists.

Passages

'A stowaway on an aircraft coming in to land at Heathrow fell
to his death in a Homebase carpark yesterday . . . It is thought
that the stowaway fell as the pilot of an unidentified jet lowered
the aircraft's landing gear. Police said the man was of
Mediterranean or Middle Eastern appearance, in his late twen-
ties or early thirties. He was wearing black jeans and a shirt and
carried no identification.' 14 June 2001, *Aviation Security
International*.

The Pomegranates of Kandahar

This poem was prompted by an item broadcast in January 2002
on BBC World Service Radio, about the legendary orchards of
Afghanistan. The very best pomegranates in the world were once
grown in profusion in Kandahar province.

Wolves Are Massing on the Steppes of Kazakhstan

Headline of a news report on BBC World Service Radio filed
on 15 January 2000 by their Central Asia Correspondent.

ACKNOWLEDGEMENTS

Acknowledgements are due to the editors of the following publications where some of these poems were first published, *Contemporary Poetry and Contemporary Science* (edited by Robert Crawford, Oxford; OUP, 2006), the *Guardian, Irish Pages, London Review of Books, Magma, New Writing 12* (edited by Diran Adebayo, Blake Morrison and Jane Rodgers, London; Picador, 2003), *101 Poets Against the War* (edited by Todd Swift, Cambridge; Salt Publishing, 2003), *Poetry Ireland Review, Poetry Review, Tall Lighthouse, The Wolf.*

'A Fistful of Foraminifera' was commissioned by Robert Crawford for the 'Contemporary Science Meets Contemporary Poetry' project supported by Stanza. The poem emerged out of a collaboration with Professor Norm McLeod, Keeper of Palaeontology at the Natural History Museum; I am deeply grateful for the encouragement, insight and information he gave me.

'The *Sand Fulmar*', 'The Foot Tunnel', 'A Village of Water' and 'The Water Diviner' were commissioned by BBC Radio 4; the programme, 'A Village of Water', was produced by Tim Dee and broadcast in February 2003.

'My Father's Piano' was commissioned by BBC Radio 3 for broadcast in the Poetry Proms series, 2000; the programme was produced by Fiona McLean. Many thanks to Stefan Jacubowski of Blüthner Pianos, Berkeley Square, London W1, who kindly dismantled an upright for me.

I am grateful to the National Endowment for Science, Technology and the Arts (NESTA) for awarding me a fellowship.